INTOXICATION

IDIOM   INVENTING WRITING THEORY

Jacques Lezra and Paul North, series editors

INTOXICATION

JEAN-LUC NANCY

Translated by PHILIP ARMSTRONG

Fordham University Press   *New York 2016*

This book was originally published in French as Jean-Luc Nancy, *Ivresse* © Éditions Payot & Rivages, 2013. The quotation from Malcolm Lowry's *Under the Volcano* is reprinted by permission of SLL/Sterling Lord Literistic, Inc., © Peter Matson.

Fordham University Press has no responsibility for the persistence or accuracy of URLs for external or third-party Internet websites referred to in this publication and does not guarantee that any content on such websites is, or will remain, accurate or appropriate.

Fordham University Press also publishes its books in a variety of electronic formats. Some content that appears in print may not be available in electronic books.

Visit us online at www.fordhampress.com.

Library of Congress Control Number: 2015935157

Printed in the United States of America

18 17 16   5 4 3 2 1

First edition

TRANSLATOR'S NOTE

The text that follows was originally read at a vineyard in Alsace in April 2008, in the town of Ribeauvillé, part of a discussion organized around the theme of intoxication.

I would like to thank Mark Bender, Jennifer Branlat, May Mergenthaler, Bert Harrill, and David Petrain, especially for help tracking down sources and quotations. I would also like to thank Tom Lay and Eric Newman for their care and help in bringing the text to publication.

In response to a number of questions, Jean-Luc Nancy offered unusually generous feedback and advice. While his suggestion to add inebriated asides to the translation was tempting, the translation seeks to remain faithful both to the spirit in which it was written and to its original layout in the edition published by Éditions Payot & Rivages. All footnotes are my own.

INTOXICATION

You must be drunk always. That is everything: the only question. Not to feel the horrible burden of Time that crushes your shoulders and bends you earthward, you must be drunk without respite.

But drunk on what? On wine, on poetry, on virtue—take your pick. But be drunk.[1]

(Thus speaks Baudelaire—perhaps we know this only too well—because, in the end, why this commandment as an exergue to modernity? Why do we need this imperative regarding intoxication if not that one perceives that it is lost, forgotten, dried up . . . ? because the "burden of Time" is felt as such, when time could be intoxication's cadence, the rhythm of impulses and torpor, of pleasures, of extravagance and calm, which make the revival of intoxications attractive . . .)

. . . .

> She will go along an uncertain path,
>
> stumbling method
>
> attempting to take a step backward
>
> toward a more originary illumination,
>
> giddiness of revelation,
>
> or of indistinction between the world and emotion

Sixteen centuries before Baudelaire, Li Bai writes in "Song of the Kingdom of Wei":

> How does one chase away the sorrow that oppresses us?
>
> Wine, wine alone has the power to do this.[2]

. . . .

At the same moment as Baudelaire, Wagner writes:

In the surging swell

in the resounding echoes

in the universal stream

of the world's respiration—

to drown one's sorrows

to sink—

unconscious—

supreme pleasure[3]

. . . .

When a discourse on intoxication is announced, one might expect either a patient analysis of the specific characteristics of this condition and its significations (enthusiasm, the Dionysian, celebration) or a passionate exaltation of excess, debauchery, distraction, and euphoria. Whether in fear or hope, this is what one expects—either a sober discourse or a drunk discourse. Sobering up or inebriation. We might even think: reason or passion, philosophy or poetry.

However, it is philosophy that says: "the True is thus a Bacchanalian revel in which no member is not drunk," just as, Hegel adds, the same truth is "transparent and simple repose."[4] But this relaxation is one of the effects of intoxication; as Hegel also states, "each of the members, in separating themselves [*sich absondert*] from others, also immediately dissolves [*auflöst*]."[5]

(Just like Hegel, Schelling also commemorates the bacchanalia of truth, and Hölderlin the *aorgic*.[6] This is the great, shared memory of the three friends from *Stift*, the Tübingen Protestant Seminary—this is their mutual baptism in a new age. One hears them inventing cabaret hymns.) All distinction and all separation is abolished, similar to Mallarmé's lace "in the doubt of the ultimate Game."[7]

Doubt suspended between distinction and dissolution, between clear figures and mixture, confusion, magma—is it reality or dream, madness or common sense?—doubt suspended in this sense could become a good method: the sly genius would be alcohol, but even though it deceives me as much as it wants, it cannot deny that *I am*, I who drinks or who believes that I'm drinking, whatever the liqueur. *Ego sum, ego existo ebrius*—I am, I exist—drunk.

This game of truth is regulated by the way the distinct, determinate, and separate—the individual; consciousness; the knotted, embroidered stitch—loses its difference in the clear tracery of the lace, which is hardly distinguishable from the background [*fond*] of velvet or silk that it adorns.

This lace, hardly distinguishable, likes to feel itself penetrating this background of felt, of sand or mud. And likes to feel itself penetrated by the individual, the consciousness—which ends up feeling like neither one nor the other but a beast, a demon, melancholy, frenzy.

❙ ❙ ❙

And so, does philosophy get drunk on poetry? Or is it the opposite? This drinking binge or banquet has taken place since both have existed.

Before, there were trances and the euphoria of sacred liqueurs. However, not every divine service is intoxication; the god needs to position itself indistinguishably between what is drunk and those that drink. The divisions and sharings between gods and worlds still had to be abolished,

> abolished and played out again
>
> in the doubt
>
> the game
>
> the abandon of projects and projections
>
> the presentation of a present.

A present where *eros* and beauty speak to each other without owing anything to each other than themselves, *eros* and beauty, Alcibiades and Diotima, the excited, the enchantress.

I | I

You will say that Socrates never gets drunk. He leaves in the morning without staggering, having drunk like none other. In truth, his intoxication precedes all others. It is immemorial. "Know yourself!"—here is the open abyss, the promised indistinction, the river without return. The oracle opens up to him the iron doors of nonknowledge. The oracle of Apollo, the Pythia or Delphic oracle herself already drunk with the smoke of laurels.

From laurels to hemlock and priestess to priestess, Socrates is by himself a Dionysian procession. He knows well that "yourself" is the other and infinity. But neither in escape nor a divine God—not *Deus absconditus*—no, here and now, the same right at [*le même à même*] its most intense exhaustion.

From Delphi to Mantineia, one has to admit that he is also a poet, this subtle rival of both Homer and Parmenides. And of a very sober Pythagoras.

❚ ❚ ❚

Thus, poetry and philosophy—both desires for intoxication, or both intoxications.

But which has drunk the other? Because to get
drunk, one has to drink. The poet can order us to
get *"drunk . . . on wine, on poetry, on virtue—take
your pick,"* but it remains—it remains even more
the case—that we need to understand how poetry
or virtue *drink*.

Now, one can drink them, of course, just as one can
drink in someone's speech. What is drinking? One
says that blotting paper soaks up ink or that salt
soaks up red wine spilled on a tablecloth. To drink
is to absorb. To be taken in, food must be first swal-
lowed, then digested. Drink, however, seems in-
stead to spread out immediately through the whole
body. It is an impregnation, an irrigation, a diffusion
and infusion. If a double symbolism of bread and
wine exists, which Christianity inherits from ancient
Dionysian, aphrodisiac cults, it stems from a double
valance—one solid and substantial, the other liquid
and spiritual.

As the Christian transubstantiation reveals (we are not distinguishing here whether in reality or figuratively), bread and wine are the body and blood. The distinction between "body" and "blood" attests to the spiritual nature of blood. Circulating throughout the body, giving it life, this blood flow is principle and vector rather than substance and organism.

The difference can be found in the words of Jesus: "This is my body given for you . . . This is my blood of the covenant, which is poured out for many . . . I tell you, I will not drink of this fruit of the vine from now on until that day when I drink it anew with you in my Father's kingdom."[8]

Blood is treated differently, much more solemnly. It is the alliance or covenant, and it is expressly the divine wine. It is the "precious water" of the Aztec sacrifice around which the four hundred gods of intoxication roam, children of agave and *pulque*.

Divinity of wine, spirit of wine, another kingdom, found elsewhere in the bottom of

> *The honest glass in which laughs the divine oblivion*

as Verlaine remarks in a poem that closes with reference to "the chalice" and "the host."[9]

However, the spirit and soul of wine is the wine itself; it is this prisoner of the bottle that is addressed to man, this other prisoner.

Again, from Baudelaire:

> *The soul of the wine*
>
> *sang by night in its bottles: "Dear mankind—*
>
> *dear and disinherited! Break the seal*
>
> *of scarlet wax that darkens my glass jail,*
>
> *and I shall bring you light and brotherhood! . . ."*[10]

. . . .

Strictly speaking, blood is not even soul—which is form and motion of the body—but *spirit*, which is intangible breath, traversing the body without inserting itself there. As one knows, it is not by chance that *spirit* names the strongest liqueurs, the *spirits of wine* or specially prepared *spirits* ready for fermentation or distillation, processes aimed at obtaining an *essence*, in other words, the pure, ideal, and reasoned [*sensée*] truth of a concrete, opaque, and perceptible substance. Spirit or liqueur, the liquidity or liquoricity of spirit represents nothing other than the perceptibility of the imperceptible, the exquisite sensuality of pure Sense—truth, transcendence, divinity, revelation, ecstasy.

One can also say that there is a spiritual stake in every drink defined with a minimum of value or sense other than a thirst-quenching function. This is symbolized in the acts of clinking glasses, making a toast, raising one's glass, drinking from the same glass, or ritually smashing a glass. Or again, through mythical or legendary figures of all kinds of *nectar* and other divine drinks poured in as many cups, hanaps, chalices, and grails, *sacred vessels* that doubly express the excellence of the drink—through the precious nature of the vessel that receives, contains, and presents it to the lips, or through the mystical content of the liquid.

The divine liquid is at once what is reserved for the gods, which is their secret, and what is offered to them. In other words, this is the blood—the sacrificial blood (to which, in many ways, fecund women were associated, givers of life) is specifically the drink of the gods, being already divine spirit in the body of men or animals. The character of effusion and infusion specific to drink leads to divine effects. The gods at once pour forth, discharge, gush, *and* the flow, flood, and outpouring *are* themselves divine.

Intoxication bears the legacy of sacrifice—communication through fluids and its outpourings, with the *sacrum*, exception, excess, outside, interdiction, the divine. In short, intoxication is the success of a sacrifice whose victim would be the sacrificer himself. Bataille recognized the ultimately comic character of the sacrificer who, at the limit, remains flawless. No doubt intoxication is also comic because the inebriate does not completely disappear, afterward feeling pitiable, sobered up, and sometimes disillusioned with intoxication itself.

That being said, the strict refusal of intoxication nonetheless expresses a refusal or even an ignorance of the existence and proximity of an outside, of a ruptured barrier through which everything can flow.

. . . .

Divinus deus (Bataille): "I decided to continue drinking and living in just this way. My whole life long."[11]

. . . .

What one calls the "body" is no more solid than what one calls the "soul" is ethereal. Their being one and the other, one in the other and one another—form everywhere spread out, extended, and the infinite palpitation of its *sameness* [mêmeté] always distorted and made thirsty [*altérée*].

> *Absolute hydra, drunk with your blue flesh,*
>
> *Forever biting your own glittering tail*
>
> *In a commotion that is silence's equal.*[12]

(Yes, the sea is always the sea that takes us over or makes us have another glass [*se reprend en nous*], the sea swell where the abyss swirls around, man's *wine-dark sea* of a thousand turns, which ceaselessly returns to the self.)[13]

The body is just as fluid and gaseous as solid. It is gaseous in the rhythmic exchange of breathing, an incessant exchange of the intangible with the intangible through the bronchial tubes and the nostrils—breath, the infrathin suspension in the most volatile state of the substance (nature, thing, the real).[14] It is fluid at the heart of this exchange, flowing through the veins in the arteries, circulating throughout, impregnating and soaking into flesh and tissue.

To which is added all the humors and secretions of the lymph, perspiration, synovial fluids, colored bile, sperms, salivas, menstruations, liqueurs of desire or drainage. The body is a field defined by spreading [*épandage*] and a network of sources, a streaming, trough, backwater, pumping, turbine, and waterworks machinery that together keep life wet—in other words, passage, permeability, sliding, floating, swimming, and bathing. It is not only in the same river that Heraclitus bathes twice; it is in the same body. He is never himself without also already being soaked in strangeness, dripping with new moisture.

The body's form—thus, the soul, the *psyche* spread out entirely in its being-there—is not only that of a statue, even if mobile and sensitive, conscious, able to feel. It is a much more complex and less-well-drawn-out form, the form of an expansive and transvasive informality, a kind of liquidity that hugs contours. No doubt each body retains the flow of all kinds of waters and oils that are not meant to flow. But in its relative closure—always relative, always open through suitable orifices—it itself never stops flowing and foundering [*couler*].

▮▮▮

Drinking is knocking back [*s'envoie*] this irrigation, this inundation. The action of drinking—gulping, a long draught, sucking in, lapping up—only quenches thirst by pouring inside oneself this liquid quality, which begins through the capacity of passing into the system (everything that is contained there) that it penetrates with and moistens in an instant, without any other law than the simple and effortless weight of mastication. And it does this in such a way that the specific contact, taste, aroma, and spirit of the drink radiates from the stomach, whether water, wine, milk, or beer.

Thus, gulping follows the throat: the open mouth and a little spillage, the tongue that at once tastes and guides what is gulped down, passing the cheeks and teeth, up to the throat, along which it is discharged, flowing toward the stomach where it foments [*fait lever*] a freshness or warmth full of fragrances and aromas, spices and sugars. But what emerges from all this fomentation [*levée*] and effervescence of crushed fruits is still something else: it is the very movement of fomentation itself. It is the impulse or yearning of a pulsation that is made known, coming from further away and moving further than any perceptible delectation. It makes sense sublime [*le sublimé du sens*], the beyond flowing in the veins—what, finally, one calls spirit.

In the most pressing sense of the word, intoxication *expresses* (which shares the same root as a press [*pressoir*] and pression). It is the juice that spreads from absorbed liqueurs. It extracts, exudes, distills— that is to say, it concentrates, warms, evaporates, and disperses [*sublime*]. What is rendered sublime is spirit, the impalpable, the immaterial. It is inspiration, breath, without place [*hors lieu*], beyond time [*hors temps*], the present concentrated in itself that one calls the *presence of spirit*—the lively, instantaneous touch of a revealed truth. Intoxication reveals—which is to say, it reveals *itself*, itself and not a secret. It reveals itself as the impetus and flight of spirit—enthusiasm, the excess [*débordement*] of knowledge, the effusion of grace. Intoxication is the condition of spirit. It makes its absoluity [*absoluité*] felt, in other words, its separation from and with [*d'avec*] everything that it is not—everything that is conditioned, determinate, relative, bound. Intoxication is itself the absolutization [*absolutisation*], unbinding, and free ascension to the world's outside. It is pleasure [*jouissance*]—identity given in abandon to the drive [*poussée*] that unbinds the identical, the body bound to its convulsions, to wrenching out a sigh or radiance, exclamation between tear and lava.

Pleasure [*Jouir*] takes place in the absolute's elsewhere, in this a-part [*à-part*] of and from everything, which is nowhere [*nulle part*]. It springs forth [*jaillit*] in this suspension that a shudder withdraws from all attachment and continuity, letting it express the absolute itself—pushing it, squeezing it outside, beyond everything and beyond itself. But this outside is disclosed as true—intoxication is this truth, the assured taste of this truth of presences that are eclipsed in their coming.

More exactly, there is thus nothing in common with fantasy, the frenzy of being transported into the possession of absoluity, sovereignty, or divinity. Neither possession of nor possession by . . . but that which does not take place, the dispersal of the place itself. The "absolute" is nothing other than (it "is" only) the dissolute, the dissolved, spilling outside.

Presences that are eclipsed in a trance, a dance, a rhythm.

. . . .

As one might expect, free falling is not far away. At the same point of the absolute where all exteriority and interiority is dissolved, excess is also produced.

One usually envisages excess as movement, transgression, overcoming [*franchissement*], leap, and impetus. But it is just as much—or even more so—a suspension, cessation, stasis, because, in fact, one does not exceed or leave the possible. The impossible is amazement and shock, not a movement that is followed. So it is for all intoxication and pleasure. Excess is an access—to the inaccessible. It accedes truly—but it is the inaccessible to which it does and does not reach. Its amazement, its trance, its tremor is truly [*proprement*] its absoluity—at once attained and reflected [*renvoyée*] to its absolute detachment.

At the same time, the excess that you have been hearing about here evokes something else—namely, the drunk rather than drinking. It is not very easy to decide between them or distinguish them. One should not be too quick to separate out a good and bad use of intoxication. There is habitual drunkenness [*ivrognerie*] in the most sublime intoxication—habitual drunkenness, in other words, dependency and degradation.

In truth, it is not easy here to tell the difference between dependency and liberation, oppressiveness and frivolity, degradation and sublimity. It is not easy separating sadness or drunken anger from Dionysian joy, which enhances whoever experiences it.

Spinoza: joy is the passage from a lower perfection to a higher perfection, and it is exactly the "perfectioning" infinity that creates the movement of the absolute, toward the absolute.

. . . .

Spinoza, "drunk from God"—*Gott trunken,* says Goethe, taken up by Novalis or Schelling.

Spinoza has drunk. He has absorbed substance— thing, nature, God. He lets himself become absorbed, inundated, irrigated, impregnated.

Near to them is Hölderlin:

> *From the thundering god issues the joy of wine.*[15]

I | I

Apollinaire:

> *Listen to my songs of cosmic drunkenness*

a line or verse that comes at the end of "The Harvest Month," the last poem in *Alcools,*

from which it is worth detaching this passage in order to read here the entire last section—after all, nothing expresses intoxication better than the ways poems are made or unmade, unknotted, untied.

The entire universe concocted in wine

Containing the oceans the animals the plants

Cities destinies singing constellations

At the riverbank of heaven kneeling men

And docile iron our dear companion

Brother fire we must love as ourselves

All the prideful dead are one beneath my brow

A flash of lightning like a thought newly born

All names by sixes all numbers by ones

Tons of paper twisted like fires

And fires that someday blanch our bones

Immortal poems suffering quietly

Armies drawn in battle formation

Forests of cruciforms and lacustrine houses

At the shore of the woman's eyes I love

The flowers crying out of mouths

And all I can never say

All I can never comprehend

All and all transformed to perfect wine

What Paris thirsts for

Was given me then

Performances lovely days unlovely sleep

Vegetation Copulation the music of the spheres

Movements Adorations divine despondency

Worlds you resemble resembling ourselves

I have drunk you and my thirst survives

But now I know the flavor of the cosmos

I am intoxicated with cosmos

*On the pier where I saw waves below the barges
sleeping*

Listen to me I am the gullet of Paris

If it pleases me I will swallow all of creation

Listen to my songs of cosmic drunkenness

And the September night ended in no hurry

The fiery bridges were doused in the Seine

*The constellations died and day had barely
begun.*[16]

. . . .

Yes, the poets are all drunk, but no less than the phi-
losophers, even if in a different way—even, and perhaps especially, in order to rediscover and repeat

Socrates, as any philosopher completely under the influence [*saoulée*] constantly reiterates.

Yes, under the influence, overwhelmed by too much knowledge, nonknowledge, virtue, mastery, dialogue, midwife, yet transported, excited, disoriented . . .

The whole of philosophy in the drunken repetition of an astonishing drinker who remains in self-control and who, in this way, passes into a higher form of intoxication.

Because he who "beat everyone" at drinking even though "no living person has even seen him drunk" (220a)—as Alcibiades remarks in *The Symposium*— he is nevertheless no less drunk of consciousness, of nonknowledge and knowledge so true that it makes us dizzy, drunk with Ideas whose design is so pure that we remain dazzled, speechless, drunk, as well as or first of all by Eros's pressure, who wants to carry off beautiful bodies until their beauty resembles "the beautiful itself, single in substance and divine" (211e).[17] He, Socrates, about whom Alcibiades will only decide to tell the truth under the influence of wine—this same wine that Socrates drinks in front of him without getting drunk—recalling at the beginning that "truth is revealed by wine and children" (217e).

The truth of wine and children is a truth neither sought nor found, which neither proves or establishes itself; it is given, fully given, given before all donation. One doesn't swim back upstream. It flows from the source, and this is how one can drink poetry or virtue—at the source, from the bottle, in a flow that owes nothing to the throat that receives it. Poetry or virtue, image or music, thought, emotion— to drink signifies to absorb, to become a sponge.

This is what happens incessantly if one considers how often this preoccupation is substituted without our knowing by tiny absences, shocks, outbursts, carried away in a fleeting moment, a taste, smell, affect, or concept. Minuscule, infinitesimal, evanescent intoxications, no less existent but that conceal us, always beginning again, covered over through preoccupation, projects, action, what confounds truth with the accomplishment of a process.

. . . .

Une pensée, un désir, un livre,

Une pincée de givre

Enivre

[A thought, a desire, a book,

A sliver of frost

Inebriates]

. . . .

The truth, the absolute truth—separation, distinct from everything. Mixed with everything and everyone as the distinctive mark of distinction itself. What we already know, that we recognize without hesitation when intoxicated—not like the stupidities that intoxication exposes us to but like intoxication itself, like inebriation.

This recalls Hegel again, whose Bacchanalian procession staggers across Socrates' sure steps.

The absolute is the separated, the distinct. Not simply the untied or detached—*solutum*—but what is completely a-part—*ab*—withdrawn and folded back on itself, self-accomplished, perfect—*perfectum*—achieved, completed, totally accomplished in and of itself. Turning around itself infinitely, vertiginously re-centering back on itself, and thus—very exactly—coming close to me, whirling around and as close as possible to my burdensome immobility.

This is inebriation—it lifts up but does not resolve itself.

Mir wirbelt der Kopf. Heißt es, das Absolute sei im Wirbel, bei mir? Oder sei vielleicht der Wirbel selbst? Vielleicht die Trunkenheit und der Wein, vielleicht in Wein aufgelöst, das Dissolutum des Absolutum?

"My head is spinning. Does this mean that the absolute would be close [*auprès*] to me in this spinning? Or that it itself would be this spinning? Perhaps dissolved in wine, *dissolutum* of the *absolutum*?"

"The absolute wants to be close to me"—these are Hegel's words. It wants and desires it. It is there already, it is always there, and it still desires it. Being close, it desires to approach. Proximity is desire to be close and is therefore not close without still approaching. Without end. The absolute is this desire, this vertigo of infinite desire. It is the whirling, exhilaration, and amazement of desire extended toward the closest proximity, toward the extremity, toward the excess of proximity, which in its excess escapes more closely than close, infinitely close, and thus always infinitesimally distant. Always more perfectly in proximity.

There is no delirium, no pretention to say that the absolute seeks to be close to us. It is only that one knows and senses it and that this has nothing to do with an overpowering paranoia. It's not about power but evidence (which is also to be understood exactly like *ego sum, ego existo*? There is no assumption of "self" here, no initiative for self-identification. This is said quite simply: I am here, here I am, whether I'm mad, asleep, or dead drunk. I am here. Nothing can be done about it). It's not serious. It's not something fundamental. It is only that nothing can be done against it. Except to say that "I is an other," but that I know as well, precisely in saying *ego sum*.

|||

Perfekt, perfect, full, integral, unconditional. Depending on nothing, having no dependency. Perfectly full of itself, saturated, soaked, drunk. *Selbstbesoffen*. The subject intoxicated [*grisé*] by itself.

Saoul—drunk—comes from *satis*, enough. *Satura* is abundant matter—mixture of fruits and vegetables, mixture of meter and genre, mixed gender, satire, miscellany, subject completely mixed up with itself, tangled in itself, gorged consciousness, overindulgent unconscious, incontinent.

Saturation detached from everything and ignoring everything, but appearing to everything, interpellating everything and everyone, everywhere intrusive and everywhere at home, taking me by the arm, the tail, hugging me, throwing me. Absolute mixed of the absolute, a mixture of the separated with the detached, confusion of distinctions.

At every step, she accompanies and stands alongside me, brushes up against me and envelops me—an accomplished plenitude that, on the one hand, leaves me missing her and wounded, disabled, myself separated from her perfect separation. But through my very separation (alone, precarious, amputated, disoriented) I participate in her separation and am penetrated by her—and here I am at home, and here I am, separated myself, absolutely! On the other hand (but I believe it is the same, the same that I see doubled), she fulfills me, drawing me toward her, bringing me closer to her as she approaches me, making me nothing other than the desire for her, her desire to be with me and my desire to be close to her—our desire as the closest proximity and vertigo of the infinitely near.

I Ⅰ I

Proximity's derivation and drift [*dérivée*]; the more it approaches, the further it moves away from what proximity promises—from *being close* [*l'auprès*] as such, from *bei*, from this "*chez*," this "domicile, at home, this homemaking, in intimacy, property, belonging, dependency, and familiarity."

(Property, proper, that which is true [*proprement*] to oneself, in itself and for itself—one knows how much this totters, how much this slips outside oneself and escapes. There is nothing drunker than the proper. However, one has to make do with this and make use of it [*en user*]—soberly, of course.)

Bei, behören, gehören—appartenir, relever de, être propre à—belong, stem from, be proper to. The absolute belongs to us, is part of us, lives with us. It is part of our domesticity, our jurisdiction, our deepest interior. And it wants it. And this is what it wants, its desire that belongs to us.

How would I not be traversed at each instance by this desire—not simply the wish to be detached—to be absolved from all ties and drunk with my detachment, fulfilled from unbinding—but desire itself as detachment, as absolution and dissolution of attachments, as intoxication of the infinite? How would the infinite not be drunk, and how would I be able not to become intoxicated?

❙ ❙ ❙

Rausch, Geräusch, rustling, roaring of the spirit's wind. Intoxication, *ebrietas,* emptied glass and inundated sense. Flow of risky drafts. Beverage, *Getränke, trinken, getrunken,* drank, *betrunken,* intoxicated. Held, penetrated, drowning in aerial or liquid impulses, in the excess of fulfillment, in the overflowing of the full.

How could plenitude not overflow itself? How could perfection not pass beyond the perfect? When one says that the glass is full, it is because it already overflows itself. Everyday French says "*être plein*"—to be full—for "being drunk." One also says "*être bourré*"— stuffed, hammered. Once again, how do we separate intoxication from habitual drunkenness?

I | **I**

The detached, *ab-solutum*, the untied or independent are in my dependencies. That's how we get drunk with one another.

The independent depends on me [*Dépend de moi l'indépendant*]. Thus, not depending, but rather I am depending on this independence whose infinite proximity appropriates me as what is more proper to me than any possible property.

Impossible property, property of the impossible. I possess it; it possesses me—the unbound binds me; its bond unties me. I am absolute, absolved, detached, untied, delivered from my faults, sins, attachments, and blemishes.

Ego te absolvo—I absolve you, I absolute you, I unbind you from all debt, dependency, even from your independence, because here you are held in my absolute dependence.

My head swims, I stagger, I swirl around, keel over.

Besoffen, full, hammered; *saufen* is the way animals drink—lapping, sucking, gorging with juice—*Saft*—*Suppe*, *soma*, or nectar of the gods, and, like them, drinking from the springs of the heavens, inhaling and sucking up the world's sap.

The absolute's long addiction [*maladie*], full like wineskin [*outre*] and overflowing, collapsing and flowing near to us, absolutely soluble in its own liqueur, in its liquidity—*Flüssigkeit*—fluidity and leakage, permanent dissolution where the absolutization of the absolute whirls and abandons itself. Abandons itself absolutely, so close to us that we are no longer distinguishable from it—the absolute absolutely distinct. We are ourselves separated from everything, beyond the world and ourselves, feeling

nauseous [*le cœur au bord des lèvres*], the heart
and thought spread out, dissolute, absolutely obso-
lete [*révolus*].

*Immer schon perfekt vollendet—bei uns wie ohne
uns.* [Always already perfectly perfect or completed—with us as well as without us.]

. . . .

To finish up, because we have to pretend to
finish up,

One has to fall asleep or ramble on a bit more,

from this long digression on intoxication, which
we are

thinking, writing, reciting,

through fiction and truth telling,

our joy, our distraction,

in order to finish up: come back to literature,

and this text from Malcolm Lowry—from *Under the Volcano*—this novel that Philippe Lacoue-Labarthe loved so much and made me imbibe or soak in:

The Consul dropped his eyes at last. How many bottles since then? In how many glasses, how many bottles had he hidden himself, since then alone? Suddenly he saw them, the bottles of aguardiente, of anís, of jerez, of Highland Queen, the glasses, a babel of glasses—towering, like the smoke from the train that day—built to the sky, then falling, the glasses toppling and crashing, falling downhill from the Generalife Gardens, the bottles breaking, bottles of Oporto, tinto, bianco, bottles of Pernod, Oxygénée, absinthe, bottles smashing, bottles cast aside, falling with a thud on the ground in parks, under benches, beds, cinema seats, hidden in drawers at Consulates, bottles of Calvados dropped and broken, or bursting into smithereens, tossed into garbage heaps, flung into the sea, the Mediterranean, the Caspian, the Caribbean, bottles floating in the ocean, dead Scotchmen on the Atlantic highlands—and now he saw them, smelt them, all, from the very beginning—bottles, bottles, bottles, and glasses, glasses, glasses, of bitter, of Dubonnet, of Falstaff, Rye, Johnny Walker, Vieux Whisky, blanc Canadien, the aperitifs, the digestifs, the demis, the dobles, the noch ein Herr Obers, the et glas Araks, the tusen taks, the bottles, the bottles, the beautiful bottles of tequila, and the gourds, gourds, gourds, the millions of gourds of beautiful mescal . . . The Consul sat very still. His conscience sounded muffled with the roar of water. It whacked and whined round the wooden frame-house with the spasmodic breeze, massed, with the thunderclouds over the trees, seen through the windows, its factions. How indeed could he hope to find himself to begin again when, somewhere, perhaps, in one of those lost or broken bottles, in one of those glasses, lay, for ever, the solitary clue to his identity? How could he go back and look now, scrabble among the broken glass, under the eternal bars, under the oceans?[18]

. . . .

WIRBEL [TURBULENCE][19]

Das Absolute ist immer schon bei uns und will bei uns sein.

[The Absolute is always already with us and
wants to be with us.]

*Immer schon? Wieso? Und bei, ganz nah, wo
denn genau? Bei uns? Bei wem denn? Und will
es? Warum? Wozu? Und wie soll denn das Absolute wollen? Wie könnte es nicht an sich bleiben?
Absolut sein heißt doch, an und in sich getrennt,
zurückgezogen zu bleiben? Heißt bleiben, nicht bei
sein. Heißt denn das Absolute nicht, was es heißt?
Ist das möglich? Ist das denkbar? Darf es sein?*

[Always already? In what way? And near or with,
very close by, where exactly? With us? With
whom exactly? And does it want to? Why? What
for? What exactly should the Absolute want? How
could it not remain in itself? Does being Absolute mean separated itself, in itself, remaining
withdrawn? Remaining means not being with.
Doesn't the Absolute mean what it means? Is this
possible? Is this thinkable? Can it be?]

Why not?

The absolute is the separated, the distinct. Not
simply the untied or detached—*solutum*—but what

is completely a-part—*ab*—withdrawn and folded back on itself, self-accomplished, perfect—*perfectum*—achieved, completed, totally accomplished in and of itself. Turning around itself infinitely, vertiginously re-centering back on itself, and thus—very exactly—coming close to me, whirling around and as close as possible to my burdensome immobility.

Mir wirbelt der Kopf. Heißt es, das Absolute sei im Wirbel, bei mir? Oder sei vielleicht der Wirbel selbst? Vielleicht die Trunkenheit und der Wein, vielleicht in Wein aufgelöst, das Dissolutum des Absolutum?

[My head is spinning. Does this mean that the absolute would be close (*auprès*) to me in this spinning? Or that it itself would be this spinning? Perhaps intoxication and wine, perhaps dissolved in wine, *dissolutum* of the *absolutum*?]

The absolute wants to be close to me. It wants and desires it. It is there already, it is always there, and it still desires it. Being close, it desires to approach. Proximity is desire to be close and is therefore not close without still approaching. Without end.

The absolute is this desire, this vertigo of infinite desire. It is the whirling, exhilaration, and amazement of desire extended toward the closest proximity, toward the extremity, toward the excess of proximity, which in its excess escapes more closely than close, infinitely close, and thus always infinitesimally distant. Always more perfectly in proximity.

▌▌▌

Perfekt, perfect, full, finished, terminated, integrated, integral, accomplished, unconditional. Depending on nothing other than itself, having no dependency, resting on itself: *substantia*. Perfectly full of itself, saturated, soaked, drunk. *Selbstbesoffen*. The subject intoxicated [*grisé*] by itself. Nothing more—no accident—can happen to it.

Saoul—drunk—comes from *satis*, enough. *Satura* is abundant matter—mixture of fruits and vegetables, mixture of meter and genre, mixed gender, satire, miscellany, subject completely mixed up with itself, mocking itself, satirical, tangled in itself, gorged consciousness, overindulgent unconscious, incontinent. Infinite irony that laughs at itself, like Menippus, the *Satyre Menippee de la Vertu du Catholicon d'Espagne et de la tenue des Estats de Paris*: "But I esteem that the name comes from the Greeks, who introduced men disguised as Satyrs onto the scaffolding used for public festivals, pretending to be lascivious and frisky demigods playing in the forests."[20]

Saturation detached from everything and ignoring everything but appearing to everything, skeptical inspector interpellating everyone, everywhere intrusive and everywhere at home, taking me by the arm, the tail, hugging me, throwing me, detaching me, taking me back. Absolute mixed of the absolute, a mixture of the separated with the detached, confusion of distinctions. K says: absolute relation of the absolute.[21]

At every step, she accompanies and stands alongside me, brushes up against me and envelops me—an accomplished plenitude that, on the one hand, leaves me missing her and wounded, disabled, myself separated from her perfect separation. But through my very separation (alone, precarious, amputated, troubled, disoriented) I participate in her separation and am penetrated by her—and here I am at

home, and here I am, separated myself, absolutely!
Me in myself displaced without being able to become an other and completely abandoning myself.
On the other hand (but I believe it is the same, the
same that I see doubled), she fulfills me, drawing
me toward her, bringing me closer to her as she approaches me, making me nothing other than the desire for her, her desire to be with me and my desire
to be close to her—our desire, right up to confusion,
as the closest proximity and vertigo of the infinitely
near. One could say pleasure [*jouissance*], but it is
more than this, because pleasure loses itself beyond
the self, whereas here everything comes back, gath-
ers together, fills up, satisfies itself, up to exhaustion.

I | I

How would I not be traversed at each instance by
this desire—not simply the wish to be detached—to
be absolved from all ties and drunk with my detachment, fulfilled from unbinding—but desire itself as
detachment, as absolution and dissolution of attachments, as intoxication of the infinite? How would the
infinite not be drunk, and how would I be able not
to get myself drunk or made infinite [*m'infinitiser*]?

What are you saying? That that will be dead only
once? Are you telling the truth? What truth? *In vino
mortis veritas in vino veritatis mors, mors stupebit*—"In wine is the truth of death, in wine is the
death of truth, death will be stupefied."[22]

❚❚❚

Rausch, Geräusch, rustling, roaring of the spirit's
wind. Intoxication, *ebrietas*, emptied glass and inundated sense. Flow of risky drafts. Beverage, intoxicated, carried away by the wave, liquidated, lique-
fied in the excess of fulfillment, in the overflowing
of the full.

How could plenitude not overflow itself? How could
perfection not pass beyond the perfect? When one
says that the glass is full, it is because it already overflows itself.

How is the body liquid? Isn't it with all its water,
blood, lymph, its genital liqueurs, its tears, its es-
sential oils, its bile or synovial humors? Doesn't the
body leak out when it no longer has to deal with
some necessity? When it floods, overflowing its own
tide?

I ‖ I

The detached, *ab-solutum*, the untied or independent are in my dependencies. That's how we get drunk and get soaked [*inondons*] with one another.

The independent depends on me [*Dépend de moi l'indépendant*]. Thus, not depending, but rather I am depending on this independence whose infinite proximity appropriates me as what is more proper to me than any possible property. *Evohe.*[23]

Impossible property, property of the impossible. I possess it; it possesses me—the unbound binds me; its bond unties me. I am absolute, absolved, detached, untied, delivered from my faults, sins, attachments, and blemishes.

What is proper? Who is proper to me? Of being susceptible of being taken hold of, stumbling, of not following my path, or of not even having one—this is what is more proper to me than any other supposedly distinct sign.

My head swims, I stagger, I swirl around, keel over.

Immer schon perfekt, vollendet—bei uns wie ohne uns. [Always already perfectly perfect or completed—with us as well as without us.]

In the Dogon tradition, making beer has been taught to man by the *bara-jile* spirits.[24] But these spirits are ambiguous; they wish both good and evil for man. With beer they have created intoxication, and with intoxication at the same time they have created rituals for sharing drinks and language as well as the possibility for angry outbursts and insults.

Shut up!

. . . .

But listen, listen having heard the Delphic paean, listen to it itself:

Bromios:

euboi!

The ground runs with milk, runs with wine,

runs with the nectar of bees.

The bacchic god holds aloft,

fragrant as smoke from Syrian incense,

his flaming pine torch

lit from the fennel wand and rushes on,

now running, now dancing,

rebuking the stragglers,

spurring them on with joyous shouts,

and tossing his luxuriant locks to heaven.

And midst his ecstatic cries he calls,

"On bacchants,

on you bacchants,

pride of the River Timolus that runs with gold:

sing Dionysus' praises

to the deep-roaring drums,

making ecstatic cries to the god of ecstasy

with Phrygian shouts and exclamations,

when the lovely pipe

shrills, all holy, its holy songs in concert

*with those who go to the mountain, to the
mountain!"*

Hence in joy

like a colt with its grazing mother,

the bacchant leaps and gambols on nimble legs.

*Enter Teiresias, identifiable by his prophetic
insignia but also wearing, somewhat
incongruously, a garment of fawnskin and
carrying a thyrsus.*[25]

Oh, the cries and songs, the dances, the excitement.
Oh, the celebrations this protesting and hurling god
gives to himself, whose voice resonates with both
complaint and joy. Whose voice reverberates on the
stage of the tragic Euripides, of Theocritus's idyll,
of André Marie Chénier, who is unable to conclude:

Come, O divine Bacchus, O young Thyoneus,

O Dionysus, Evan, Iacchus, and Lenaeus;

Come, like you appear to the wilderness of
Naxos,

When your voice reassures the daughter of
Minos . . .[26]

—to Nietzsche in front of the crucifixion:

Nicht lange durstest du noch,

verbranntes Herz!

Verheißung ist in der Luft,

aus unbekannten Mündern bläst mich's an,

—die große Kühle kommt . . .

[You shall not thirst much longer,

scorched heart!

A promise is in the air,

from mouths unknown it wafts to me

—great coolness comes . . .]²⁷

. . . and the agitated music on the stage of "Las Ménades" ("The Maenads") by Julio Cortázar . . .²⁸

*No doubt nothing is revealed at the extremity of
intoxication than intoxication itself.*

What is this nothing? What thing? What disaster?

Hölderlin:

. . . from the Indus

Young Bacchus came, with holy

Wine rousing the peoples from sleep:

*O you also, poets, you also awaken!*²⁹

. . . .

the sumptuous, howling, flowing spectacle
of the bacchic procession where the name of
Bacchus is shouted out—sound, recitation,

all this spectacle engenders the spectacle in its
entirety,

intoxication of showing oneself and of seeing
oneself showing oneself,

same dizziness,

vertigo of visibility [*paraître*] and offering
oneself to be seen,

of making the outside burst forth [*jaillir*]

being no more than extremely outside oneself

insolent coming into being [*venue au jour*]

Thus, in *The Seagull*, Nina Mikhailovna Zarechnaya
says:

> *I'm a real actress. I enjoy acting, I adore it. I am*
> *intoxicated on stage, I feel I'm beautiful.*[30]

Or else, or else the young girl who is drunk that Raskolnikov wants to save.[31]

ENVOI

Prince, and you illustrious drinkers,

You may remember to drink to my,

For the same,

The time that is given you to live

And he, eternally drunk,

Where you are rendered to the world's turbulence

. . . .

drunk lucid as much as empty glass

clear presence a pure existence that disappears in its appearance

nothing other than a flash of lightning between two clouds

where my lucidity would not be if

my delirium was less whole

and less widely disoriented

. . . .

"Unfortunately the coefficient which thus alters our values alters them only during that hour of intoxication" (Proust, *Within a Budding Grove*).[32]

"Oh, I know somebody's going to quote Augier at me: 'What matters the bottle so long as one gets drunk?' Well, Robert may have got drunk all right, but he certainly hasn't shown much taste in his choice of bottle!" (Proust, *The Guermantes Way*).[33]

NOTES

1. Charles Baudelaire, "Get Drunk" ("Enivrez-vous"), in *Paris Spleen: Little Poems in Prose*, trans. Kcith Waldrop (Middletown, Conn.: Wesleyan University Press, 2009), 71.

2. The poem may be attributed to Li Bai. It dates from the Tang dynasty.

3. These are the closing lines of Richard Wagner's opera *Tristan and Isolde*. Nancy translates the German *ertrinken* as *s'enivrer*, thus drawing out the sense of intoxication implied in drowning one's sorrows in drink.

4. G. W. F. Hegel, *Phenomenology of Spirit*, trans. A. V. Miller (Oxford: Oxford University Press, 1977), 27. Nancy remains closer to the German than the existing English translations. See G. W. F Hegel, *Phänomenologie des Geistes*, in *Werke* (Frankfurt am Main: Suhrkamp, 1970), 3:46.

5. Ibid. Translation modified.

6. Nancy is punning here on Hölderlin's references to the *aorgisch* or "aorgic," which Hölderlin opposes to the organic. See Friedrich Hölderlin, "Ground for Empedocles," in

Essays and Letters on Theory, trans. Thomas Pfau (Albany: SUNY Press, 1987), 50–61.

7. Stéphane Mallarmé, "Lace Sweeps Itself Aside" ("Une dentelle s'abolit"), in *Collected Poems*, trans. Henry Weinfield (Berkeley: University of California Press, 1994), 80.

8. Matt. 26:28 (New Revised Standard Version).

9. Paul Verlaine, "Wisdom" ("Sagesse"), in *Selected Poems*, trans. C. F. MacIntyre (Berkeley: University of California Press, 1948), 169.

10. Charles Baudelaire, "The Soul of Wine" ("L'ame du vin"), in *Les fleurs du mal*, trans. Richard Howard (Boston: Godine, 1982), 113.

11. Georges Bataille, "My Mother," in *My Mother/Madame Edwarda/The Dead Man*, trans. Austryn Wainhouse (London: Marion Boyars, 1995), 61. *Divinus Deus* is the title Bataille gave to a proposed collection of texts, including *Madame Edwarda*, *Ma mère*, *Charlotte d'Ingerville*, and *Sainte*. See Georges Bataille, *Œuvres complètes IV*, *Œuvres littéraires posthumes* (Paris: Gallimard, 1971), 169–311.

12. Paul Valéry, "The Graveyard by the Sea" ("Le cimetière marin"), in *Poems: The Collected Works of Paul Valéry*, trans. David Paul (Princeton, N.J.: Princeton University Press, 1971), 1:221.

13. "Man's *wine-dark sea* of a thousand turns" is an expression from Homer's *Iliad* and *Odyssey*. "A thousand turns" also echoes Odysseus's famous epithet, *polytropos*,

"of many turns" (Nancy thus transfers the epithet from the man to the sea on which he travels).

14. *Inframince*—usually translated as "infrathin"—is an expression coined by Marcel Duchamp.

15. Friedrich Hölderlin, "Bread and Wine" ("Brod und Wein"), in *Poems and Fragments*, trans. Michael Hamburger (London: Anvil Press Poetry, 1994), 271. Translation modified.

16. Guillaume Apollinaire, "The Harvest Month" ("Vendémiaire"), in *Alcools: Poems*, trans. Donald Revell (Hanover, N.H.: Wesleyan University Press, 1995), 168–171.

17. All translations of *The Symposium* are taken from Plato, *The Symposium*, trans. M. C. Howatson (Cambridge: Cambridge University Press, 2008).

18. Malcolm Lowry, *Under the Volcano* (New York: Harper & Row, 2014), 377–378.

19. *Wirbel*—spinning, whirling, turbulence—is a term that appears in the writings of both Hegel and Heidegger. The following section was first published in French in a slightly different form in Thomas Strässle and Simon Zumsteg, eds., *Trunkenheit: Kulturen des Rausches* (Amsterdam: Editions Rodopi, 2008), 11–13. The following sections and quotations are thus Nancy repeating and (mis)quoting himself from this earlier publication. This earlier publication is not noted in the original French version of *Ivresse*.

20. *La satyre Ménippée de la vertu du catholicon d'Espagne* was a political satire written in French in 1593.

21. K is a reference both to the protagonist in Kafka's *The Trial* as well as [Søren] Kierkegaard.

22. Nancy's phrase is a parody of the proverb *in vino veritas*—"in wine there is truth"—followed by a tag from the *Dies Irae*, "mors stupebit et natura,/cum resurget creatura/iudicanti responsura"—"Death will be dumbstruck, and nature too, when creation will rise again to give answer to the judge."

23. *Evohe* or *euhoi* is a bacchic cry in praise of Dionysus.

24. See Éric Jolly, *Boire avec esprit. Bière de mil et société dogon* (Nanterre: Publications de la Société d'ethnologie, 2004), 228ff.

25. Euripides, *Bacchae*, trans. David Kovacs, Loeb Classical Library (Cambridge, Mass.: Harvard University Press, 2002), 23–25.

26. André Marie Chénier, an eighteenth-century French poet of Greek origin, whose poem "Bacchus" is included in "Bucoliques. Idylles et fragments d'idylles." See *Poésies choisies de André Chénier*, ed. Jules Derocquigny (Oxford: Clarendon, 1907), http://www.gutenberg.org/files/17899/17899-h/17899-h.htm.

27. Friedrich Nietzsche, "The Sun Sinks" ("Die Sonne sinkt"), in *Dithyrambs of Dionysus (Dionysos-Dithyramben)*, trans. R. J. Hollingdale (London: Anvil Press Poetry, 1984), 48–49.

28. See Julio Cortázar, "Las Ménades" ("The Maenads"), in *Final del Juego* (Mexico: Los Presentes, 1956), 60–83. The Maenads were the female followers of Dionysus.

29. Friedrich Hölderlin, "The Ister" ("Der Ister"), as quoted (in part) in Martin Heidegger, *Hölderlin's Hymn 'The Ister,'"* trans. William McNeill and Julia Davis (Bloomington: Indiana University Press, 1996), 7.

30. See Anton Chekhov, *The Seagull,* in *Five Plays,* trans. Ronald Hingely (Oxford: Oxford University Press), 114 (in Act IV). Translation modified.

31. Rodion Romanovich Raskolnikov is the protagonist in Fyodor Dostoyevsky's *Crime and Punishment.* Toward the beginning of the novel, he encounters a young girl who is staggering down the street, drunk, perhaps having been raped.

32. Marcel Proust, *Remembrance of Things Past,* vol. 1, *Within a Budding Grove,* trans. C. K. Scott Moncrieff and Terence Kilmartin (New York: Vintage, 1982), 874.

33. Marcel Proust, *Remembrance of Things Past,* vol. 2, *The Guermantes Way,* trans. C. K. Scott Moncrieff and Terence Kilmartin (New York: Vintage, 1982), 235. The quotation is from Alfred de Musset, not Augier.

IDIOM   INVENTING WRITING THEORY
Jacques Lezra and Paul North, series editors